ANIMALS ATTACK!

Bears

Gail Jarrow

KH

**KIDHAVEN
PRESS™**

THOMSON

—★—

GALE

San Diego • Detroit • New York • San Francisco • Cleveland
New Haven, Conn. • Waterville, Maine • London • Munich

THOMSON
GALE

™

Picture Credits

Cover: © Getty Images
© W. Perry Conway/CORBIS, 38
COREL Corporation, 35, 37
© DiMaggio/Kalish/CORBIS, 34
© Lowell Georgia/CORBIS, 18
© Dan Guravich/CORBIS, 35 (inset)
Chris Jouan, 6, 17
© Mark Matheny, 31
© Joe McDonald/CORBIS, 20
Brandy Noon, 10
© Richard T. Nowitz/CORBIS, 40
PhotoDisc, 14
© D. Robert & Lorri Franz/CORBIS, 29
© Galen Rowell/CORBIS, 5, 15, 25, 30
© Gordon & Cathie Sullivan/AnimalsAnimals/Earth Scenes, 14 (inset)
© Kennan Ward/CORBIS, 9, 24
© Steffan Widstrand/CORBIS, 26, 39

LIBRARY OF CONGRESS CATALOGING-IN-PUBLICATION DATA

Jarrow, Gail.
  Bears / by Gail Jarrow.
    p. cm.—(Animals attack)
Summary: Discusses reasons why bears attack and relates stories about
such attacks.
  ISBN 0-7377-1525-1 (hardback : alk. paper)
1. Bear attacks—Juvenile literature. [1. Bear attacks. 2. Bears.]
I. Title. II. Series.
  QL737 .C27J37 2003
  599.78'15—dc21
2002013083

Printed in China

Contents

Chapter 1

The Attacking Bear

A grizzly bear charges its victim at thirty miles per hour, faster than an Olympic sprinter. When the bear gets close, it roars and rises on its hind legs. The towering bear stands at more than seven feet, taller than a basketball star. Its three-inch claws and sharp teeth flash as it prepares to attack.

Survivors of bear attacks never forget this image. For some attack victims, it is the last thing they will ever see.

A Mighty Fighter

Three types, or species, of bears live in North America: the brown bear (often called the grizzly bear), the

American black bear, and the polar bear. All three bear species use their teeth and claws to attack enemies or prey. A bear is so strong that even a slap with its paw can cause injuries requiring medical attention.

The sheer size of an attacking bear puts a human at a disadvantage. When standing upright, the average male grizzly stands six to seven feet tall and weighs 500 pounds. The average male black bear

A massive grizzly bear rises on its hind legs and lets out a loud roar.

How Big Is a Bear?

	7-year-old	Rugby Player	Black Bear	Polar Bear
	50 lbs	225 lbs	350 lbs	1,000 lbs

10 feet
9 feet
8 feet
7 feet
6 feet
5 feet
4 feet
3 feet
2 feet
1 foot

weighs 350 pounds and is five or six feet tall. An average male polar bear weighs nearly 1,000 pounds and stands eight to ten feet tall. Some bears are even larger. Female bears are usually smaller than males.

Bears are speedy, too. It is impossible to outrun one. Bears can sprint at thirty to thirty-five miles per hour, far faster than any human. In fact, running away from a bear can trigger its chase instinct and cause it to attack.

Some people think they can escape an attacking bear by climbing a tree. But black bears are excellent climbers and will follow a human up a tree. Although adult grizzlies do not usually climb trees, they have been known to climb up almost thirty feet to grab a person.

Risk of Attack

Experts estimate that North American bears kill an average of three people a year and seriously injure fewer than a dozen. Considering that millions of people visit bear territory each year, this is a small number.

A person has a greater chance of dying from many other causes. For example, from 1839 to 1994, bears in Yellowstone National Park killed five people, far fewer than park deaths from drownings, falls, or vehicle accidents.

Glacier National Park in Montana has the highest concentration of grizzly bears south of Canada. Many of the park's 2 million visitors camp and hike in grizzly bear areas every summer. Yet bears injure only one or two people a year. From 1913 to 1995, Glacier National Park grizzlies killed only nine people.

Polar bear attacks are rare and occur most often at hunting camps, research stations, and towns. One study in Alaska counted incidents from 1900 to 2000 in which a bear threatened a person. Out of 475 dangerous meetings between bears and humans, only 6 involved polar bears. In Canada, which has more polar bears than Alaska, polar bears caused only fifteen injuries and four deaths between 1970 and 1985.

Human–Bear Encounters

A person's chance of meeting a bear depends on where he or she lives and travels.

More than fifty-five thousand grizzly bears live in the wilderness of Canada and Alaska. Only about one thousand grizzlies still remain in the lower forty-eight states—in Montana, Wyoming, Idaho, and Washington—where the grizzly is listed as a threatened species.

Black bears are usually found in forests. Biologists estimate that more than six hundred thousand black bears live in the United States, Canada, and Mexico.

The polar bear population in the icy Arctic is difficult to count. Wildlife experts estimate that about five thousand polar bears live in Alaska and more than fifteen thousand live in Canada.

The number of human–bear encounters has increased as more hikers and campers visit bear **habitats**. In fact, most bear attacks occur in national parks during the summer months. In some parts of North

Curious polar bears investigate a protective cage used by researchers.

America, housing developments have expanded into black bear territory, further increasing the contact between bears and humans.

Fortunately, people are not likely to be attacked by a bear, even if they hike and camp. Bears usually avoid humans and are not aggressive toward them. In most human–bear encounters, the bear seems to ignore people. Or it might investigate, then run away.

How Deadly?

Grizzly bears are the most dangerous of the three North American bear species. These mighty bears are strong enough to move granite boulders weighing several hundred pounds. Half of all grizzly bear attacks on humans result in either a major injury or death. The grizzly's attack is so devastating because the bear often grabs the person's neck or head with its teeth. That is the same way it kills deer, moose, and elk. During the twentieth century, grizzlies killed about eighty people in North America.

Black bears are less aggressive than grizzlies. Despite being far more numerous than grizzly bears, black bears caused only thirty-five deaths in North

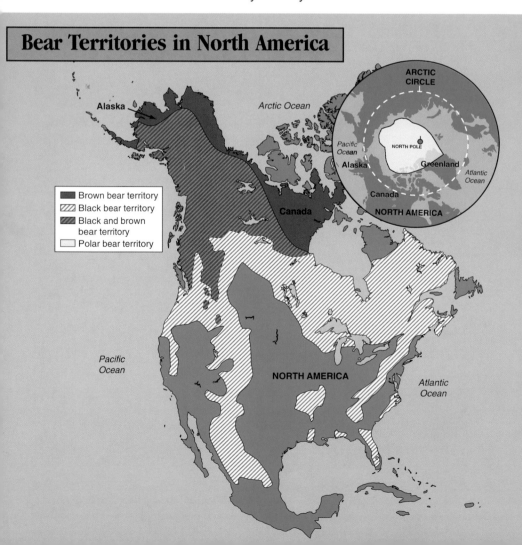

Bear Territories in North America

America from 1900 to 2000. A black bear is powerful enough to bite through a tree thicker than a man's arm. Yet it rarely uses this strength against people. When black bears do attack, they usually cause minor injuries. In one study of North American bear attacks between 1960 and 1980, black bears injured about five hundred people. But less than 10 percent of the injuries were serious.

Experts believe that when a bear attacks a human, it is usually caused by one of three reasons.

Surprise!

Surprise is the most common reason for bear attacks. A person catches a bear off guard by coming too close to it or by blocking its travel route. This makes the bear feel that it is in danger, triggering the animal's defensive behavior.

Mothers with Cubs

If a person approaches a mother bear with cubs, the female may attack to protect her young. She reacts defensively because she feels threatened. Such attacks occur even when the person has not separated the cubs from their mother, but has merely come close to them. Some female bears are more aggressive when they have young cubs.

Bears that Hunt Humans

The least common reason for bear attacks is an aggressive **predatory bear**. The bear acts as a

predator, attacking for food and intending to eat the human.

Although grizzly and black bears get most of their nourishment from plant material such as berries, nuts, and roots, they also prey on animals. This sometimes includes humans. Polar bears eat mostly meat, with seals being their primary food. When other food is scarce, polar bears occasionally prey on humans.

Bears can lose their natural fear of people if they begin to associate humans with food. This happens when people feed bears or when campers are careless with food. The bears may then approach humans, sometimes aggressively and often causing injuries and damage to property.

After the Attack

After an attack, a bear often runs off and is never found. Officials post bear warnings near the attack site so that future hikers and campers will be alert. Park trails may be closed if the danger is thought to be too great.

The Forest Service and National Park Service try to trap and relocate bears that regularly come too close to humans. If a bear is extremely aggressive, it may have to be killed. But these actions come too late for victims of a bear attack.

Surprising
the Bear

A hiker comes around a bend in a trail and meets a bear. The bear has not heard, seen, or smelled the person approaching. Such an encounter rarely results in a serious injury. The bear usually runs away once it realizes that it is not in danger.

But individual bears react differently, depending on their personality and previous experiences with humans. A bear may attack if its defensive reaction is triggered.

The Shepherd's Story

Kathryn Clausen worked as a shepherd in British Columbia, Canada. In June 1999, she was walking

Grizzly bears use their sharp claws (inset) for attacking prey, as well as for walking on difficult terrain, climbing, and protection.

back to camp at the end of the day with three herding dogs. As they turned a bend on a wilderness road, Clausen spotted two adult grizzly bears half a football field away from her.

She stopped, waiting for the bears to leave. The grizzlies sniffed the air, then stepped toward her. The dogs barked wildly. Suddenly, the larger bear charged her.

In a flash, Clausen sprinted away. She heard the bear grunting as it closed the distance between them. Knowing that she could not outrun the grizzly, she headed for a nearby tree. With the bear at her heels, she leaped for the lowest limb and pulled herself up.

Dogs to the Rescue

Without hesitating, the grizzly started up the tree after Clausen. It swiped at her with its claws as she scrambled through the limbs. The three dogs were close behind, jumping and snapping at the bear's rear end. The bear backed down the tree to chase the dogs, giving Clausen a chance to climb higher.

For fifteen minutes, the dogs' barks and nips distracted the grizzly and prevented it from snatching Clausen from the tree. The attack ended when her coworker arrived with

A chained sled dog attacks an intruding polar bear.

several more dogs. The two grizzlies retreated, apparently because they were outnumbered.

Clausen was lucky. She had just enough head start on the charging bear to climb a tree to safety. Thanks to the herding dogs, the grizzly never climbed high enough to reach her.

Skiing into Trouble

Jim "Ole" Olson encountered a grizzly while working at Wyoming's Grand Teton National Park. As he skied to a patrol cabin one March night in 2001, he noticed grizzly tracks in the snow. But he saw no bears. Later, as he crossed an open meadow, Olson realized that a bear was right behind him.

While trying not to panic, he crouched down and turned toward the bear. His headlamp's light revealed an adult grizzly about twenty yards away. Without warning, the bear charged and attacked, biting Olson on his shoulder and rear end. The attack lasted only a few seconds, and then the bear strode away.

Olson lay still for five minutes. When he was sure the bear was gone, he got up and skied to the cabin. Fortunately, Olson's only injuries were a torn arm muscle and some bite wounds. After surgery to repair the damage, he fully recovered.

Park rangers investigated the attack the next day. Snow tracks showed that the grizzly had been traveling at the edge of the woods near the meadow. When Olson appeared, the bear attacked him, perhaps believing that the man presented danger.

Built to Attack!

Massive, wide skull with broad nostrils and large jawbone hinge.

Forty-two teeth, including sharp canines for hunting and defense, as well as flat, strong molars for crunching and grinding.

Long snout with prominent nose for excellent sense of smell.

Agile forepaws capable of moving small objects with great precision.

Sharp claws and thick footpads for running, hunting, and climbing.

Ability to stand upright for increased sight distance.

Because Olson did not move during the attack, the grizzly might have thought that it had killed him. The bear ended its attack quickly and moved on.

Interrupting a Bear's Meal

Patricia Van Tighem and Trevor Janz were not as lucky. They surprised a grizzly bear at the worst time—while it was eating. According to a bear attack expert: "One of the most dangerous situations in which to come nose to nose with a grizzly is when it is feeding on or is near a carcass."[1]

In September 1983, Van Tighem and Janz were backpacking in Waterton Lakes National Park, Canada. Janz was hiking ahead of Van Tighem when he saw a bear a dozen yards off the side of the trail. Although Janz did not know it, the grizzly had been feeding on a bighorn sheep carcass.

A hungry polar bear inspects a whale carcass. Bears can be very aggressive while feeding.

"All I saw was a brown flash to the side. I had a second to turn away and then she was on me,"[2] recalled Janz.

Before Janz could react, the bear grabbed his leg and pulled him down. As the young man fell, he landed on his face with his hands under his body. His bulky backpack provided some protection against the attacking grizzly. The bear mauled him for a minute or two, growling and grunting as it bit the man's body.

Then the bear abruptly left. It had spotted Van Tighem.

Not High Enough

When Van Tighem saw the bear attacking Janz, she ran for a tree. After climbing up about sixteen feet, she looked down.

Van Tighem described what happened next:

I freeze. Terror fills me. It's right there. Eye contact. Small bear eyes in large brown furry head, mouth open. It's charging the tree. A scream, loud. It's moving so incredibly fast. . . . It launches itself at the tree. Three huge lunges, branches flying and cracking. . . . Brown ball of muscle and fury. . . . Knocks the branch out from beneath my feet. Swats at my leg.[3]

As Van Tighem fell from the tree to the ground, she used her hands to protect her head. She rolled on her front, playing dead. The bear kept up the attack.

A hiker scrambles up a tree to escape an angry grizzly bear.

"A grizzly is chewing on my head. Crunch of my bones. Slurps. Heavy animal breathing. . . . Jaws around my head."[4]

Finally in desperation, Van Tighem worked her fingers free. She reached up and tweaked the bear's nose. The animal backed off.

"I Was Sure She Would Kill Me"

But the attack was not over. After leaving Van Tighem, the grizzly returned to Janz. The man had gotten to his feet after the initial attack and had started to climb a tree to safety. He had climbed only about five feet when the bear pulled him down.

This time Janz's head was not protected from the bear's bites. "She [the bear] got me by the back of the neck and threw me back and forth. She hurt me the most that time. I was sure she would kill me."[5]

Finally, the bear stopped its attack and ran off. Ten minutes later, two hikers came down the trail. They managed to carry the critically injured couple three miles to medical help.

Janz suffered damage to his jaw and facial nerves. Van Tighem's injuries were even more serious, including the loss of her eye. She endured more than a dozen surgeries to repair her injuries.

Why So Vicious?

Park wardens, accompanied by bear expert Stephen Herrero, searched the mauling site the day after the attack. They found the sheep carcass and bear tracks.

While they were investigating, a female bear broke through the trees and charged the men. As the grizzly lunged toward one of the wardens, he shot and killed her with his rifle.

Afterward, Herrero wrote: "Sometimes such encounters at carcasses can be anticipated and avoided, but this time there were no good clues to suggest the possibility of a carcass or an attack. Fortunately, such incidents are very rare."[6]

Make Some Noise

Bear attacks such as these can often be avoided if the bear is not surprised. Park rangers tell hikers to make noise as they walk on forest trails. The bears hear people approaching and are not caught off guard.

Approaching a Mother Bear

A female bear, called a **sow**, has a strong instinct to protect her young. The mother may attack a person who comes close to her cubs, especially if she feels threatened. The cubs often stay hidden during the attack.

Two Against One Grizzly

Dr. Barrie Gilbert went to Wyoming's Yellowstone National Park in June 1977 to study grizzly bear behavior. He hoped attacks could be prevented if bear behavior was better understood.

Early one morning Gilbert and his assistant, Bruce Hastings, watched through binoculars as a

These grizzly bear cubs stay close to their mother, careful not to wander far from her protective reach.

male and a female grizzly with three cubs fed in a grassy area. After two hours, the researchers headed to higher ground where they could observe the bears from a different angle.

When Gilbert and Hastings reached the new location, the male was still in the grassy area, but the female and her cubs were gone. The men hiked along a ridge, hoping to see the sow and cubs in another meadow. As

Gilbert lifted his binoculars, he suddenly heard a grizzly's "woof" and saw fur coming at him.

Not Fast Enough

Gilbert tried to give the sow as much room as possible. He ran toward a small tree, but the bear caught him before he could climb it.

"The bear started biting me on the back of the head, which felt like a pick-axe scraping along my skull bones,"[7] he reported later. He tried to kick the bear away, but instead of leaving him alone, the grizzly bit his face and leg.

An animal trainer plays dead during a safety demonstration with a captive grizzly bear.

Black bear cubs follow a hiker through a meadow. Mother bears may attack if they feel their cubs are in danger.

Meanwhile, Hastings had been fifty feet behind Gilbert on the trail. When he heard the bear attacking, he hurried to a clump of trees and shouted. The sound was enough to frighten away the bear. Using their radio, Hastings called for a helicopter and then administered first aid.

The sow had caused severe injuries by attacking Gilbert's head. His facial bones were crushed, and he lost his left eye. The wounds required plastic surgery and more than a year of recovery.

Because the men had been hiking quietly, they probably surprised the mother grizzly. Feeling threatened, she charged.

A Black Bear Sow Attacks

Like grizzlies, black bear mothers are protective of their young. Jimmy Biagiona saw this firsthand in May 1999 while working for the Ministry of Forests in British Columbia, Canada.

One day he was inspecting logging work with his sixty-five-pound dog Bandit, a coyote-shepherd cross. As Biagiona emerged from a stand of trees, he noticed a female black bear with two small cubs. They were at a safe distance—more than a football field away. Biagiona called out so that the bears would not be surprised. In the past, bears had always wandered away when they heard him call. Not this time.

The sow ran full speed toward Biagiona. He shouted, hoping that she would stop. But she kept coming. Without wasting another second, he sprinted in the opposite direction.

He heard the bear's growls and felt her paws swiping the air as she gained on him. When he looked over his shoulder to see how close she was, he tripped on a pile of debris. Falling to the ground, he landed on his face just as the bear reached him. Terrified, he waited for the bear's claws and teeth to sink into his flesh.

Brave Bandit

Bandit rushed to the scene when he saw Biagiona in danger. The sow swiped at the nipping and barking dog. With the bear distracted, Biagiona jumped to his feet and found a piece of wood. When the bear charged him again, he hit her head with it.

The blow stopped the bear for a few moments. Then she turned her attention back to Bandit. Bear and dog chased each other in circles. Biagiona grabbed another piece of wood. He moved into position and smacked the sow on her snout.

This time the blow stunned her, and the dazed bear stumbled. Biagiona and Bandit slowly backed away. Once they were out of her sight, they ran for their truck.

Not the Bear's Fault

While safely in the truck, Jimmy examined his injuries. The bear's claws had left two gashes on his hand and scratches on his forearm. Bandit's belly and shoulder had puncture wounds. Fortunately, none of the wounds was serious.

"If it wasn't for Bandit, that bear would've been totally focused on me," Biagiona said later. "I don't blame the sow for her actions, as she was just being a good mother. But she's probably got a migraine headache and a sore butt about now."[8] Biagiona, thankful for his dog's help in fighting off the bear, treated Bandit to a steak.

A Dangerous Trail

T.J. Langley, an experienced backpacker, was not afraid of bears. He figured that if he left them alone, they would leave him alone. But as a precaution, he took along a can of **pepper spray** when he headed into Yellowstone National Park in September 1999.

An animal trainer, dressed in protective clothing, sits motionless during a training session with a captive black bear and coyote.

This bear's sharp claws and huge teeth make the animal a fierce predator.

Pepper spray burns a bear's eyes, mouth, and nose, and usually makes it back off. Langley kept his pepper spray on his pack's chest strap.

As he hiked through dense timber, he spotted two small grizzly bears only twenty yards away. They had appeared suddenly. Langley decided to keep moving down the trail away from them.

When he glanced back to see where the bears were, he got a shock. A larger bear was speeding down the trail toward him. Langley suspected that it was the small bears' mother. He reached for his pepper spray, fumbling with the safety clip. Before he could shoot the spray, the grizzly attacked.

Attack to the Head

As the bear knocked Langley down, he turned his backpack around. He hoped that it would protect his chest. But the sow went after his head, trying to crush it. Langley heard the bones in his face cracking and the bear's teeth scraping against his skull.

He screamed as the grizzly ripped off his pack and flipped him over. In a last-ditch effort to save his life, Langley pushed his hand against the sow's throat. At

Blood oozes from a man's wounds after a bear attacked him.

that moment, he heard what he thought were the sounds of the two cubs. The mother hurried away.

Miles from Help

The attack had taken less than a minute. But it had left Langley with crushed facial bones and deep cuts across his head and side. He crawled back to the trail, calling out in case another hiker was nearby. But Langley was alone—4 1/2 miles from the nearest road. He could barely walk because the bear had broken off the top of his hipbone.

After nearly two hours of painful hiking, Langley made it to the road and flagged down a car. A helicopter flew him to a hospital, where he underwent many hours of surgery.

Park Service investigators later studied the attack scene. They concluded that Langley had surprised a sow and two cubs. In the heavily wooded area, man and bears had not seen each other until they were dangerously close. The sow, probably feeling threatened, had attacked.

No Warning

A female bear protecting her cubs can be extremely aggressive. The presence of a human can trigger a dangerous attack that comes without warning.

The Predatory Bear

Predatory attacks by bears are rare, but they can be fierce. Some experts believe that predatory bears have learned to associate humans with food. They invade campgrounds in search of food. These food searches sometimes lead to attacks on people. In other cases, the bear is extremely hungry and turns to human meat for food.

Yukon Grizzly

During the summer of 1999, Phil Vermeyen and Bruce (Ole) Ohlson, both experienced outdoorsmen, set off on a four-week canoe trip in the Yukon, Canada. One morning, Ohlson awoke to Vermeyen's scream.

33

A family of black bears sifts through garbage at a campsite. Bear attacks often occur when bears enter campgrounds in search of food.

A grizzly bear had pounced onto Vermeyen's tent. As the bear ripped the tent, Vermeyen tried to crawl out the opening. But the grizzly pinned him with its paw and bit into the man's back.

Ohlson grabbed his pepper spray and hurried toward the grizzly. When he was a yard away, he blasted the bear with the spray. The grizzly released Vermeyen, who scrambled away. Before the bear could follow, Ohlson sprayed it again.

The grizzly reared on its hind legs. Ohlson had only one shot of spray left. He raised his arms and yelled at the bear. "The bear turned and dropped to all fours," Ohlson recalled. "It shot a glance at me

Although polar bears depend mostly on seals for food (inset), they will occasionally approach campsites in search of something to eat.

over its shoulder; I again urged it to depart, and it ambled upstream."[9]

Escape

Blood oozed from the bite wounds on Vermeyen's back and side. The men knew that they had to get away before the bear returned. They ran for their canoe and set off downriver to the nearest town, one hundred miles away.

Luckily, after paddling six miles, the two men came to a riverside camp with a radio. A helicopter arrived to airlift Vermeyen to medical care. It took twenty stitches to close up his wounds. The bear's teeth had barely missed his lung and kidney.

Later, a conservation officer investigated the attack. He concluded that the grizzly had wandered into the camp searching for food. The two men had carefully stowed their food sixty feet from their campground so that it would not attract bears. But the grizzly came anyway. Once the bear discovered Vermeyen, it took a test bite. The taste of blood may have set off the bear's instinct to kill.

Polar Bear Attack

Four Canadian campers had a similar encounter with a polar bear in July 2001. Although polar bear attacks are rare, predatory bears caused most of the attacks recorded in Canada from 1970 to 1985.

The four campers were awakened during the night by a polar bear scratching at one of the tents. As the bear ripped open the tent, the two campers inside tried to get out the other end. Before Alain Parenteau could escape, the bear slashed him with its claws. As the young man kicked, the bear bit his thigh.

His three friends yelled and threw rocks at the bear. It suddenly charged Patricia Doyon. While the bear clawed her head, back, and thigh, Eric Fortier pulled out his pocketknife and stabbed the bear's throat. The bleeding bear stopped mauling Doyon and ambled away.

Fearing that the bear might return, the campers jumped into their canoes and paddled to the nearest town. There, Doyon's and Parenteau's wounds were stitched.

Attacks like that often occur because the bear is hungry. Polar bears depend primarily on seals for food. In the summer and fall, food is harder to find. Starving bears may approach humans.

Although bears usually avoid people, encounters like this can be dangerous.

A large polar bear investigates a tundra buggy filled with tourists.

A Hungry Polar Bear

In the fall of 1983, Fred Treul was in Manitoba, Canada, watching bears from a **tundra buggy**. That day the people in his tour group had counted more than forty polar bears. One of the bears was a thin male in poor condition. Treul thought no more about the bear as he took photographs of **tundra** wildlife.

A short time later, Treul opened the buggy's sliding window to take a photograph of a bird. As he leaned out with his camera, the same **emaciated** polar bear jumped out from underneath the tundra buggy. The bear bit down on Treul's arm and tried to yank him out the window.

Fighting Back

Another passenger punched the polar bear's nose. But the bear did not give up. "The bear had my left elbow in his mouth," reported Treul, "and was jerking me hard against the window frame."[10] The other passenger kept hitting the bear's nose, and it finally let go. The bear's powerful jaws had ripped skin and muscle in Treul's arm.

Bad weather prevented an aircraft rescue. Treul almost bled to death during the hazardous fourteen-hour ride through a blizzard to safety. Doctors saved

A photographer snaps a photo of a polar bear. Bear attacks can occur when people visit bear habitats.

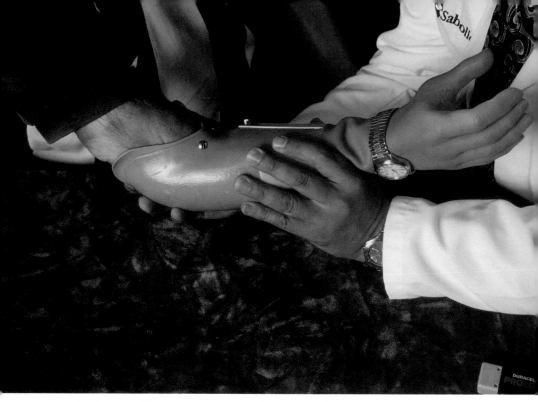

A doctor fits a patient with an artificial arm. Injuries from bear attacks can cause serious harm.

his arm. He was lucky. Two days after his encounter, a man was killed by a polar bear in the same area.

"I'm Being Eaten by a Bear!"

Black bears rarely cause serious injuries during attacks on humans. But in most of the cases in which a person died from a black bear attack, predatory bears were responsible. It was a predatory bear that attacked Cynthia Dusel-Bacon in 1977.

Dusel-Bacon, a geologist, was studying rocks in the Alaskan wilderness, where bears are common. She always clapped as she walked. This had kept bears away—until that August day.

Dusel-Bacon had stopped on a slope to examine a piece of rock. Suddenly, a black bear rose from the brush ten feet below. Cynthia shouted, trying to chase the bear off.

Thrown to the Ground

Instead of running away, the bear lunged at Dusel-Bacon. "I felt myself being thrown forward," she remembered, "and I landed face down on the ground, with my arms outstretched."[11]

Dusel-Bacon remembered that playing dead was supposed to make an attacking bear lose interest. She did not know that playing dead might not work with predatory bears. The black bear bit into her shoulder. "After playing dead for several minutes, I came to the horrible realization that the bear had no intention of abandoning its prey,"[12] she recalled.

She heard the bear's teeth biting into her skull. As she lay there wondering how long it would take to die, the bear grabbed her right arm in its jaws. Then it dragged her down the hill over rocks and brush.

Calling for Help

Somehow, Dusel-Bacon managed to use her free arm to reach for the walkie-talkie in her backpack. Holding the radio to her mouth, she called to her coworker, "Come quick, I'm being eaten by a bear."[13]

The attack continued for another ten minutes until Cynthia heard the whir of a helicopter circling above. As the helicopter circled close to the ground, the bear ran off.

"I remember the feeling of relief and thankfulness that swept over me when I found myself in that helicopter," said Dusel-Bacon later. "Deep down, though, I knew . . . that I had been too badly hurt for my body to ever be the same again."[14] She lost both arms and was fitted with artificial limbs.

People who survive a predatory bear attack feel the terror of knowing that a powerful predator wanted them for dinner.

An Unforgettable Experience

Bears inspire fear and awe. Although they normally avoid humans, attacks occur when the paths of bears and people cross unexpectedly. Yet bear attacks are rare, even in national parks, where people are most likely to encounter a bear.

People who have been attacked by a bear often suffer serious injuries. This is especially true in grizzly and polar bear attacks because these bears attack the head. The animals' strength, sharp claws, and deadly bite can cause major damage.

People who escape a bear attack with few, if any, injuries are the lucky ones. Some of them did the right thing at the right time. Some were saved by a friend—human or dog. None will ever forget the attack by a bear.

Notes

Chapter 2: Surprising the Bear

1. Stephen Herrero, *Bear Attacks—Their Causes and Avoidance.* Piscataway, NJ: Winchester Press, 1985, p. 31.
2. Quoted in Patricia Van Tighem, *The Bear's Embrace.* New York: Pantheon Books, 2001, p. 123.
3. Van Tighem, *The Bear's Embrace,* pp. 17–18.
4. Van Tighem, *The Bear's Embrace,* p. 18.
5. Quoted in Van Tighem, *The Bear's Embrace,* p. 124.
6. Herrero, *Bear Attacks,* p. 34.

Chapter 3: Approaching a Mother Bear

7. Quoted in Herrero, *Bear Attacks,* p. 20.
8. Quoted in James Gary Shelton, *Bear Attacks II—Myth and Reality.* Hagensborg, British Columbia: Pallister Publishing, 2001, p. 115.

Chapter 4: The Predatory Bear

9. Quoted in Shelton, *Bear Attacks II,* p. 81.
10. Quoted in Charles T. Feazel, *White Bear.* New York: Henry Holt, 1990, p. 146.
11. Quoted in Herrero, *Bear Attacks,* p. 111.
12. Quoted in Herrero, *Bear Attacks,* p. 112.
13. Quoted in Herrero, *Bear Attacks,* p. 112.
14. Quoted in Herrero, *Bear Attacks,* p. 114.

Glossary

carcass: The dead body of an animal.

emaciated: Starved to near death.

habitat: The natural environment where an animal lives.

pepper spray: A repellant made from hot peppers. It burns the eyes, nose, mouth, and skin of bears.

predator: An animal that hunts other animals for food.

predatory bear: A bear that hunts humans as a source of food.

sow: A female bear.

tundra: A treeless plain in arctic regions.

tundra buggy: A bus-like vehicle used by tour groups to observe arctic wildlife.

For Further Exploration

Books

Kathy Feeney, *Black Bears*. New York: Creative Publishing International, 2000. Find answers to fascinating and fun questions about black bears, including some little-known facts.

Dagmar Fertl, Michelle Reddy, and Erik D. Stoops, *Bears*. New York: Sterling Publishing, 2000. Information about the world's bears is presented in a question-and-answer format.

Dorothy Hinshaw Patent, *Great Ice Bear*. New York: Morrow Junior Books, 1999. Read about the life cycle of the polar bear and its relationship with humans throughout history.

Alvin Silverstein, Virginia Silverstein, and Laura Silverstein Nunn. *The Grizzly Bear (Endangered in America)*. New York: Millbrook Press, 1998. This book explains why grizzly bear populations have declined and what people are doing to save this magnificent animal.

Lynn M. Stone, *Grizzlies*. Minneapolis, MN: Carolrhoda Books, 1993. Find out how the grizzly bear hunts, mates, raises cubs, and communicates.

Websites

American Bear Association (www.Americanbear. org). A good site to find photographs and information about bears of the world. The Kids' Pages section contains a quiz about black bear diet and behavior. Try the jigsaw puzzle.

Animal Planet (www.animal.discovery.com). This site contains general facts, photos, and entertaining video clips about black, grizzly, and polar bears. Take the bear quiz and see how much you know.

National Wildlife Federation (www.nwf.org). Find out details about bear habitats and why the world's bear populations are threatened.

National Geographic (www.nationalgeographic. com). Watch video clips of grizzly and polar bears in the wild. Hear bear sounds, and learn fun facts. Send a bear postcard to a friend.

North American Bear Center (www.bear.org). This site has photographs and detailed information about black, grizzly, and polar bears. The Kids' Area includes slides, sounds, and facts about black bears.

Index